FRESH STRENGTH FOR THE

Grieving Heart

JENNIFER O. WHITE

All Scripture references are New Living Translation.

Editor: Rebecca LeCompte
Cover Design: FJ Designs
Formatting: FJ Designs
ISBN: 978-0-9991161-1-1
Date of Publishing: August 2019

What a treasure *Fresh Strength for the Grieving Heart* will be for anyone walking the journey of grief and loss. So often words fail us as we stumble through this journey and our hearts cannot find the words to cry out in prayer. This wonderful book provides beautiful prayers and healing scriptures to guide us along the way. I am grateful for a tool to share with others who are hurting.

Cindy Cameron
Grief Support Group Facilitator

What a great resource! As a counselor, I try to point my clients to resources that can help them through difficult seasons. This is such a book!

Jennifer White writes with an empathetic and personal experience perspective to provide real hope and encouragement to those going through the difficult season of loss. I highly recommend it!

Gil Martin
Marriage Coach for the Smalley Institute, Professional Counselor

"Every broken heart longs for comfort and solace from loss that invades our lives. In *Fresh Strength for the Grieving Heart*, Jennifer has a beautiful way of pointing people to God and His Word as our greatest source for consolation. He is our fountain for drawing deep water that heals the soul and mends our hearts. This little book is a treasure for the grieving heart; offering hope and encouragement for those suffering from any form of loss."

Angela Bisignano, Ph.D.
Psychologist and Author, Beautifully Gifted

Those who are grieving deep, immeasurable losses, including the death of a spouse or child, are in daily need of strength that can be given only by our heavenly Father. Often the one in deep grief cannot speak the prayers they need in order to sustain daily life. Jennifer has a heart and mind of prayer and has chosen the words that will bring peace and healing to those grieving such painful losses. This book will become a lifeline in your time of crisis and will serve as a daily reminder of God's loving presence and strength in your life. I love this book so much. I keep a printed copy of it on my desk and use it daily -- like I would use a vitamin -- to give me strength and guide me into purpose."

Clara Hinton, author of Child Loss - the Heartbreak and the Hope, Silent Grief, and Hope 365: Daily Meditations for the Grieving Heart.

INTRODUCTION

SECTIONS:

Dear Grieving Heart,

I am so sorry you are hurting.

I am no stranger to grief. I know it unexpectedly blows into our lives like a tornado stirring up our emotions and challenging our grip on life. The devastating things life deals us can bring everything we thought we knew about ourselves, our future, and our God into question.

Maybe your grief came with the death of someone, the loss of a dream, a separation from someone you treasured, the traumatic loss of material blessings, an abrupt change in your health, or something equally as difficult. As I write this little book, I'm working through the grief of a second failed marriage. I've watched my dad and a good friend take their last breaths after horrific illnesses. There is so much about processing grief that I don't know. What I do know is that God is more powerful than loss. I am convinced of His power to redeem our lives from the pit. He is faithful. He has overcome the world. He leads us from glory to glory. (Psalm 103:4; 2 Timothy 2:13; John 16:33; 2 Corinthians 3:18)

The Bible promises that God is close to us when we are brokenhearted. It also promises that Jesus' mission as our Savior includes healing our broken hearts. The very Word of God is like a medicine, which is well able to heal us and deliver us from evil. The Holy Spirit draws from the unlimited resources of heaven to empower us with inner strength! (Psalm 34:18; Isaiah 61:1; Psalm 107:20; Ephesians 3:16)

In the midst of your grief, I am inviting you on a journey of praying simple prayers to help you connect to who God is and what He can do. Each prayer is accompanied by the Scripture(s) revealing His promises and provision. The prayers are divided into four main themes leading you to cry out to God for help, rehearse His goodness to you, practice thanksgiving, and declare His promises as your own.

These prayerful moments with God can be the catalyst for healing, breakthrough, and blessing. You can use them as prompts for longer conversations with God about your life. You can pick out the prayers and verses that meet you where you are today and focus on them until you are ready to move on. My hope is that they will help you boast about your weaknesses to God so that His great power can come to rest on you there. (2 Corinthians 12:9)

God is our source of new mercies and fresh strength. Hard days like these will pass and we will find ourselves stronger, braver, and even more confident in the goodness of our God. (Lamentations 3:22-23; Isaiah 40:29)

With hope,

Jennifer O. White

SECTION 1
Cry Out for Help

God, I feel
so weak and
powerless
in this situation.
I am in desperate need of
Your strength.

"David was now in great danger
because all his men were very bitter
about losing their sons and
daughters, and they began to talk of
stoning him. But David found
strength in the LORD his God."

1 SAMUEL 30:6

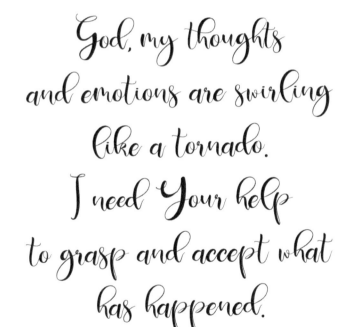

God, my thoughts
and emotions are swirling
like a tornado.
I need Your help
to grasp and accept what
has happened.

"For the LORD grants wisdom! From his mouth
come knowledge and understanding."

PROVERBS 2:6

God, my heart feels shattered and empty. I need Your healing power.

"He heals the brokenhearted and bandages their wounds."

PSALM 147:3

God, I feel so tired and weary. I am desperate for the rest only You can supply.

"Then Jesus said, 'Come to me, all of you who are weary and carry heavy burdens, and I will give you rest. Take my yoke upon you. Let me teach you, because I am humble and gentle at heart, and you will find rest for your souls.'"

MATTHEW 11:28-29

God, I am filled with anger and disbelief. I need to hear Your gentle words. Help me to speak wise and gentle words to others.

"Some people make cutting remarks, but the words of the wise bring healing."

P R O V E R B S   1 2 : 1 8

"Gentle words are a tree of life; a deceitful tongue crushes the spirit."

P R O V E R B S   1 5 : 4

*Help me,
God, to pour out my heart
to You, so I can live free
from bitterness, rage,
and slander.*

"Get rid of all bitterness, rage, anger, harsh words,
and slander, as well as all types of evil behavior."

E P H E S I A N S   4 : 3 1

"O my people, trust in him at all times. Pour out your
heart to him, for God is our refuge."

P S A L M   6 2 : 8

God, help me to guard my heart, so I am not easily offended by people who say the wrong things or avoid me because they are not sure what to say.

"Guard your heart above all else, for it determines the course of your life."

PROVERBS 4:23

"Sensible people control their temper; they earn respect by overlooking wrongs."

PROVERBS 19:11

God, help me express what I need. I want to avoid the trap of expecting people to read my mind and automatically know what I need.

"Now go! I will be with you as you speak, and I will instruct you in what to say."

EXODUS 4:12

"...for the Holy Spirit will teach you at that time what needs to be said."

LUKE 12:12

*Deliver me,
Lord,
from the fear
of*

————————————.

INSERT YOUR FEAR IN THE PRAYER

"I prayed to the LORD, and he answered me.
He freed me from all my fears."

P S A L M   3 4 : 4

Rehearse God's Goodness

God, my heart feels like shattered glass. My spirit is crushed, but You are here to rescue me from the weight of despair.

"The LORD is close to the brokenhearted; he rescues those whose spirits are crushed."

PSALM 34:18

"To all who mourn in Israel, he will give a crown of beauty for ashes, a joyous blessing instead of mourning, festive praise instead of despair. In their righteousness, they will be like great oaks that the LORD has planted for his own glory."

ISAIAH 61:3

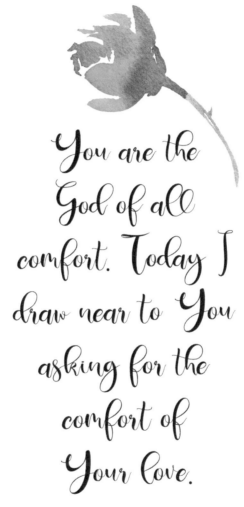

You are the God of all comfort. Today I draw near to You asking for the comfort of Your love.

"God is our merciful Father and the source of all comfort."

2 CORINTHIANS 1:3B

"But as for me, how good it is to be near God! I have made the Sovereign LORD my shelter, and I will tell everyone about the wonderful things you do."

PSALM 73:28

God, I choose to cling to Your Word, because It brings me hope. Let Your truth revive and comfort me.

"Your promise revives me; it comforts me in all my troubles."

P S A L M   1 1 9 : 5 0

"If your instructions hadn't sustained me with joy, I would have died in my misery."

P S A L M   1 1 9 : 9 2

God, this tragedy feels as if it changes everything. However, I remind myself that You are unchanging and always faithful.

"If we are unfaithful, he remains faithful, for he cannot deny who he is."

2 TIMOTHY 2:13

"Understand, therefore, that the LORD your God is indeed God. He is the faithful God who keeps his covenant for a thousand generations and lavishes his unfailing love on those who love him and obey his commands."

DEUTERONOMY 7:9

God, sometimes my heart is so heavy I feel unable to breathe. Let Your powerful breath renew my life.

"For the Spirit of God has made me, and the breath of the Almighty gives me life."

JOB 33:4

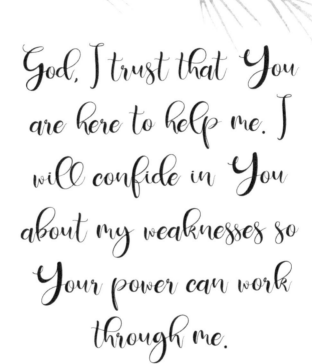

God, I trust that You are here to help me. I will confide in You about my weaknesses so Your power can work through me.

"But God is my helper. The Lord keeps me alive!"

P S A L M   5 4 : 4

"Each time he said, 'My grace is all you need. My power works best in weakness.' So now I am glad to boast about my weaknesses, so that the power of Christ can work through me."

2   C O R I N T H I A N S   1 2 : 9

I trust You, God, to bless me with all that I need because You have promised to bless those who mourn.

"God blesses those who mourn, for they will be comforted."

M A T T H E W 5 : 4

"And this same God who takes care of me will supply all your needs from his glorious riches, which have been given to us in Christ Jesus."

P H I L I P P I A N S 4 : 1 9

God, at times I feel
as if I am walking
through a dense fog.
I choose to trust that
You are always
here to guide me.

"Yet I still belong to you; you hold my right hand. You guide me with your counsel, leading me to a glorious destiny."

PSALM 73:23-24

"The LORD says, 'I will guide you along the best pathway for your life. I will advise you and watch over you.'"

PSALM 32:8

God, I am so
weary of being
sad day after
day. Yet,
I will wait
patiently
trusting You to
renew my
physical and
emotional strength.

"But those who trust in the LORD will find new strength.
They will soar high on wings like eagles. They will run and
not grow weary. They will walk and not faint."

ISAIAH 40:31

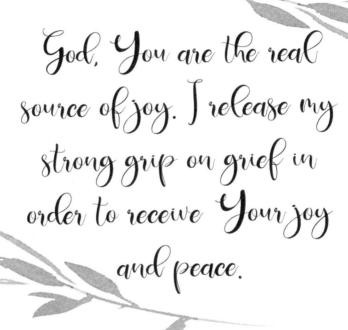

God, You are the real source of joy. I release my strong grip on grief in order to receive Your joy and peace.

"But the Holy Spirit produces this kind of fruit in our lives: love, joy, peace, patience, kindness, goodness, faithfulness, gentleness, and self-control. There is no law against these things!"

GALATIANS 5:22-23

"I pray that God, the source of hope, will fill you completely with joy and peace because you trust in him. Then you will overflow with confident hope through the power of the Holy Spirit."

ROMANS 15:13

God, You are good to those who suffer. I place my hope in Your mercy and kindness.

"We give great honor to those who endure under suffering. For instance, you know about Job, a man of great endurance. You can see how the Lord was kind to him at the end, for the Lord is full of tenderness and mercy."

JAMES 5:11

"When Job prayed for his friends, the LORD restored his fortunes. In fact, the LORD gave him twice as much as before!"

JOB 42:10

SECTION 3

Practice Thanksgiving

Thank You, God, for being with me now to strengthen me as I mourn this loss. I am so glad I am not alone.

"She will give birth to a son and will call him Immanuel (which means 'God is with us')."

ISAIAH 7:14B

"Don't be afraid, for I am with you. Don't be discouraged, for I am your God. I will strengthen you and help you. I will hold you up with my victorious right hand."

ISAIAH 41:10

Thank You, God, for pursuing me today with gifts of Your unfailing love and goodness towards me.

"Surely your goodness and unfailing love will pursue me all the days of my life, and I will live in the house of the LORD forever."

PSALM 23:6

God, I am thankful You care about my emotions. I am comforted to know every tear that I cry is important to You.

"You keep track of all my sorrows. You have collected all my tears in your bottle. You have recorded each one in your book."

P S A L M   5 6 : 8

God, I am
grateful You
know what I
need before I
ask You.

"...your Father knows exactly what you need even
before you ask him!"

MATTHEW 6:8B

Thank You,
God, for being a
very safe place
to express my
anxious thoughts.

"Give all your worries and cares to God, for he cares about you."

1 PETER 5:7

"I pour out my complaints before him and tell him all my troubles."

PSALM 142:2

"Give your burdens to the LORD, and he will take care of you. He will not permit the godly to slip and fall."

PSALM 55:22

Thank You, God, for offering me Your strength and Your protection while I am so emotionally drained and vulnerable.

"The LORD is my strength and shield. I trust him with all my heart. He helps me, and my heart is filled with joy."

PSALM 28:7A

"God dwells in that city; it cannot be destroyed. From the very break of day, God will protect it."

PSALM 46:5

Thank You, God,
for carrying my
burden of grief
and heartache.

"He was despised and rejected--a man of sorrows, acquainted with deepest grief. We turned our backs on him and looked the other way. He was despised, and we did not care. Yet it was our weaknesses he carried; it was our sorrows that weighed him down. And we thought his troubles were a punishment from God, a punishment for his own sins!"

ISAIAH 53:3-4

Thank You, God, for Your good plans to get me through this and to use me to comfort others who are hurting.

"All praise to God, the Father of our Lord Jesus Christ. God is our merciful Father and the source of all comfort. He comforts us in all our troubles so that we can comfort others. When they are troubled, we will be able to give them the same comfort God has given us."

2   C O R I N T H I A N S   1 : 3 - 4

*Thank you, God, for
Your power to help me
put away thoughts of
despair and hopelessness.*

"We destroy every proud obstacle that keeps people from
knowing God. We capture their rebellious thoughts and teach
them to obey Christ."

2 CORINTHIANS 10:5

Thank You, God, for loving me and enabling me to continue to love others. I don't want my heart to grow cold.

"Dear friends, let us continue to love one another, for love comes from God. Anyone who loves is a child of God and knows God."

1 JOHN 4:7

"And may the Lord make your love for one another and for all people grow and overflow, just as our love for you overflows."

1 THESSALONIANS 3:12

Thank You, God,
for forgiving me.
Help me to forgive

_____.

INSERT THE NAME OF SOMEONE YOU
NEED TO FORGIVE.

"Instead, be kind to each other, tenderhearted, forgiving one
another, just as God through Christ has forgiven you."

E P H E S I A N S   4 : 3 2

"But when you are praying, first forgive anyone you are holding a grudge
against, so that your Father in heaven will forgive your sins, too."

M A R K   1 1 : 2 5

// PRACTICE THANKSGIVING

SECTION 4
Declare His Promises

You, God,
are my glorious strength.
It pleases You to make
me strong! Hallelujah!

"You are their glorious strength. It pleases you to make us strong."

PSALM 89:17

My victory and honor in this life come from You alone, God!

"My victory and honor come from God alone. He is my refuge, a rock where no enemy can reach me."

P S A L M   6 2 : 7

"Instead of shame and dishonor, you will enjoy a double share of honor."

I S A I A H   6 1 : 7 A

"But you, O LORD, are a shield around me; you are my glory, the one who holds my head high."

P S A L M   3 : 3

God, You are the One
who satisfies my soul.

"You satisfy me more than the richest feast. I will
praise you with songs of joy."

PSALM 63:5

God, you remain the strength of my heart! You are mine forever.

"Whom have I in heaven but you? I desire you more than anything on earth. My health may fail, and my spirit may grow weak, but God remains the strength of my heart; he is mine forever."

PSALM 73:25-26

By Your grace, God,
this season of my life
will make me strong
and able to produce a
great harvest for Your
kingdom. Hallelujah!

"Those who plant in tears will harvest with
shouts of joy."

PSALM 126:5

"But blessed are those who trust in the LORD and have made the
LORD their hope and confidence. They are like trees planted along a
riverbank, with roots that reach deep into the water. Such trees are
not bothered by the heat or worried by long months of drought.
Their leaves stay green, and they never stop producing fruit."

JEREMIAH 17:7-8

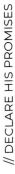

I will keep my eyes fixed on You, God, and Your good plan for my life.

"Look straight ahead, and fix your eyes on what lies before you."

P R O V E R B S   4 : 2 5

"'For I know the plans I have for you,' says the LORD. 'They are plans for good and not for disaster, to give you a future and a hope.'"

J E R E M I A H   2 9 : 1 1

God, I am grateful this season of my life is bringing a greater understanding of You. I want it to make me more like You.

"So all of us who have had that veil removed can see and reflect the glory of the Lord. And the Lord--who is the Spirit--makes us more and more like him as we are changed into his glorious image."

2 CORINTHIANS 3:18

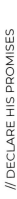

God, I cling to You and Your way in this difficult time knowing I will receive Your blessings.

"True humility and fear of the LORD lead to riches, honor, and long life."

PROVERBS 22:4

"Fear the LORD, you his godly people, for those who fear him will have all they need. "

PSALM 34:9

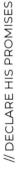

God, You are able to satisfy all my needs, so I have no need to worry.

"...and human hands can't serve his needs--for he has no needs. He himself gives life and breath to everything, and he satisfies every need."

ACTS 17:25

"Don't worry about anything; instead, pray about everything. Tell God what you need, and thank him for all he has done."

PHILIPPIANS 4:6

God, I am expecting great things to come since the resurrection power of Jesus is at work in me.

"The Spirit of God, who raised Jesus from the dead, lives in you. And just as God raised Christ Jesus from the dead, he will give life to your mortal bodies by this same Spirit living within you."

R O M A N S   8 : 1 1

"Now all glory to God, who is able, through his mighty power at work within us, to accomplish infinitely more than we might ask or think."

E P H E S I A N S   3 : 2 0

Even now, I choose to be strong and courageous because You, God, are making a way for me.

"So be strong and courageous! Do not be afraid and do not panic before them. For the LORD your God will personally go ahead of you. He will neither fail you nor abandon you."

DEUTERONOMY 31:6

A Prayer for Us

Almighty God,

We come before Your throne in the mighty name of Jesus who carried our sorrows to the cross. We invite You to pour out wisdom and revelation in the knowledge of You upon us as we walk through a very difficult season. We believe You are able to help us.

Please help us express our thoughts and feelings to You. Help us to think and act in agreement with Your perspective of what has happened. Help us choose forgiveness over and over so our hearts are free to experience Your love and express Your joy.

Thank You for making Your unlimited wealth and resources available to us through Christ. Thank You for the healing power of Your Word working in our lives. We trust these prayers are in agreement with Your Word and therefore will be very fruitful. We believe the Scriptures we have read in this book are alive and at work right now to revive our hearts.

Awaken us to Your unmatched strength and power. Show us how You triumph over every devastating work of the evil one. Breathe on the shattered places of our hearts. Let Your abundant love grow and overflow within us so our days ahead are far greater than the former ones.

You are the well of living water. Our thirsty souls gladly receive the refreshing strength of Your life today.

In Jesus' name we pray,

Amen

JENNIFER O WHITE
Jenniferowhite.com

**He sends forth His word and heals them and rescues them
from the pit and destruction. (Psalm 107:20)**

The enemy of my soul has attempted many times to destroy me. For many years, I didn't understand the spiritual battle. I will never stop thanking God for the Christian counselor He put in my life to help me apply His Word to my painful situations. I learned to pray in agreement with His Word and my journey of true healing began.

My first two books were written as a result of the radical change God made in my heart toward my husband and marriage. *Prayers for New Brides and Hope for Your Marriage* are filled with the wisdom and scriptural prayers God gave me during that season of my life.

Today, I am walking with God through a very painful divorce. He continually supplies me with fresh strength as I grieve the loss of the marriage and family I treasured. He is more than enough for me. He is the perfect place for my pain, my questions, my confusion, my anger, and my fear.

I will spend all my days exploring His faithfulness and celebrating His perfect power to supply every need. I invite you to join me in this journey of seeking Fresh Strength from God. You will find more of my books and articles to help you experience the healing power of God's Word at my website: Jenniferowhite.com

Made in the USA
Middletown, DE
03 September 2023